THE
WORLD'S
LAST
NIGHT

THE
WORLD'S
LAST
NIGHT

poems by
Margot Schilpp

For Daniel —
Thanks for
being a good student
and an even better
writer

Best —
Margot

Carnegie Mellon University Press
Pittsburgh 2001

ACKNOWLEDGMENTS

Acknowledgment is due the following magazines where poems first appeared, often in somewhat different versions:

American Letters & Commentary: "In Memory of Freud"
The Chrysalis Reader: "A Nap Sounded Good" (under the title "Napping")
Connecticut Review: "One Sunday Each Spring" and "To a Friend Who Moved Away"
Crab Orchard Review: "Vanishing Point"
Crazyhorse: "Proper Subjects" and "Intuitive Motions"
Denver Quarterly: "Triage"
Gettysburg Review: "Non Sequitur"
Green Mountains Review: "The Fish Channel" and "Hearsay"
The Journal: "Manifesto"
LIT: "A Few Cows in a Landscape"
Many Mountains Moving: "Under the Scorpion's Heart"
Meridian: "Antithesis: The Garden of Hysteria"
New England Review: "Obsessional"
Shenandoah: "Cure Porches"
The Southern Review: "Permanent Record"
Sundog: "Auto-Pilot"
Verse: "Thera"

"Devotions in Confidence," "Triage," "Under the Scorpion's Heart," and *"Non Sequitur"* appear in *American Poetry: The Next Generation,* eds. Gerald Costanzo and Jim Daniels (Carnegie Mellon University Press, 2000); "Manifesto" and "Poem from Across the Country" will appear in *American Diaspora: Poetry of Exile,* eds. Ryan G. Van Cleave and Virgil Suarez (University of Iowa Press, 2000). "In Memory of Freud" was featured on *Poetry Daily* (http://www.poems.com) on January 9, 2000; "On the Nature of Interrogatives" was published in *SLOPE* (http://slope.org), Issue 6; "In Which I Time-Travel at the End of the Twentieth Century" was published in the "Editor's Picks" section of *Web Del Sol,* May, 1999 (http://www.webdelsol.com); "One Sunday Each Spring" was reprinted in *You Can Write Poetry: A Primer,* ed. Jeff Mock, (Writer's Digest Books, Inc., 1998); "The Fish Channel" was reprinted in the *1997 Anthology of Magazine Verse and Yearbook of American Poetry* (Monitor Books, Inc., 1997) and in *Valparaiso Poetry Review* (http://www.valpo.edu/english/vpr/); "Project Cover-Up" appears in *What There Is: The Crossroads Anthology* (Crossroads Urban Center, 1996) to benefit efforts against Salt Lake City area hunger.

Publication of this book is supported by a grant from the Pennsylvania Council on the Arts.

Library of Congress Control Number 00-132937
ISBN 0-88748-348-8 Pbk.

Contents

For my parents

MADELON GOLDEN SCHILPP
and
PAUL ARTHUR SCHILPP

with deepest gratitude
and love

What if this present were the world's last night?

—JOHN DONNE, Holy Sonnets XIII

RED-WINGED BLACKBIRD

The barbed wire bends across the field
like a hair out of place, though not exactly.
The platinum sky is bleak and it weeps: gray
all day isn't the only way of grieving.
Longing is a knife that blunts itself

on the dull muscle of the heart. It's a cadaver
that seeks you in a dream. I'm razoring
my hair, cutting unruly curls which fall,
rest in the sink like faraway birds.
I'm wondering what separates hunger

from oblivion, and why this poem keeps
wanting to be about filling things, about
things emptied or combined: apple to pie,
ink to paper, distance to love. Whoever
taught me that the outer life was to be

as detached from the self as a suburban garage?
Who pointed out the beautiful markings of birds?
Summer's curtain draws across, red-winged
blackbirds weave into the fence, drag
a crimson thread across the eye.

I'm still living in a swamp, learning
the shapes of reeds. The fence
is a fishnet stocking that guards
the meadow's shapely leg.
A persistent observer can imagine contour,

the promise of naked winter.
What's happened to engineering,
caress of drawing and function?
Everyone suspects depth
is just an ivory-colored dream.

This is still about breadth, about what matters.
This is pinning a butterfly to velvet
and proclaiming it truth. When you step back
to admire the silver rod piercing the thorax,
truth matters. You won't see it there.

A bomb is just a miracle turned backwards,
a map only a suggestion-box of lines.
Years ago, after the blackbirds, I found
what I was looking for inside a gold ring,
under generous eaves. The rain smoothed

down the tiles like icing. I wanted heat.
Maybe you saw me dissolving
in the platinum rain, or touching the grass
to discover the time. It was the hour
of the pearl and the highball, or the hour

of the hankie and tear. It is always
the hour of thinking myself into the dark
wings, a little bruised from beating too long
into the fence's sheer destruction,
and too strong not to try.

ON THE NATURE OF AMBER

This necklace needs restringing, needs wire
and a clasp, needlenose pliers to secure

the ends, but I've never been skilled
at mechanical things, with sequences

and instructions, though there's something
enchanting about arranging the beads,

small to smaller to smallest, that makes sense
as rain makes puddles, spreading across

the road, larger than the potholes
they fill. To photograph the reflections

of trees in water, set the camera
on infinity. That's how far away

the image is from being captured,
from ever being caught. I do have talents.

I can take anything apart: a shoelace knot,
a rifle. I cannot dismantle

this color—wolf's eyes shot in creamy light,
where nothing can prevent refraction,

just as nothing can stop
a heart as well as the force

that makes it beat: electricity notched
up and spun though skin, a defeat

or jump-start to the circuit, just as
amber contains history and prophecy at once:

trees slid into decay, hardened into gem.
The rest is written inside, in the fissures,

like those webbing our brains, our dishes,
our land—it's a manual to tell us how we mustn't

crave beauty, another hard-to-capture fuel
that burns when you bring it close to fire.

Auto-Pilot

So many conflagrations, so many surprised
retinas, so many faces the color of a pan

left on the stove and heated to dry,
the orange of a postcard sunset,

the orange of a burning cross,
even when accompanied by the flames'

whispers, the wish of the dollhouse
burning, our screams let out the sides

of our mouths to suggest distance,
or the dark fire raging up the vein after

the plunger's depressed. These are
the burnings I remember, brief and

spectacular lights, the real heat that comes
from fuses, from the sparkling rockets

igniting the spider's web. There is light
here, then gone, a wash of lit silk,

and if the slow fever of a life relies
on brightness to create the moments

when soaring is a possibility, why complain?
Why not cast the doused rag, the straw,

the cold lump of your heart
into the flames and see what catches fire?

PROPER SUBJECTS

Take that, and that, as if striking were
the only way to get the point across.
But only one particular blue can tame me
and there is sassafras tea steeping
on the porch, a wide-planked affair clamping
three sides of the house that absorbs
the whole family's secrets.
                              The world
doesn't want to know anyway, everyone
hustles to set up the folding chairs
while you're wearing another groove
in the pine and thinning the seat's fabric.
Think of a prison
                   of metal objects: scissors,
wedding ring, Mazda, oven. First haircut,
the cellophane tape pressed against my forehead
and my mother staring just above my eyes.
The straight bangs she wants to trim.
The flyswatter falls like a drawbridge.
Foil candy wrappers shine. You can see
why we desire them—magpies searching
through the slag
                 for shine, for bright
permanence and decorations. Chain-links suspend
a swing, ratchet the rider closer, then farther
from the dark. What does oxidation tell you?
Hold this spoon in your hand—trace it
back centuries—discern the need of those
who died for history to also feed themselves.
Unless you were drawn
                        and quartered, mounted
on metal and pulled apart to prove a point,
your settlements have been made.

                                And can't I
put anything into this poem? Elmer's glue, sticks
of dynamite, a lathe, underwear embroidered
with the days of the week? Who'll stop me?
I'm a steam-engine, a force—tornado,
cyclone, tsunami, flood. Either you believe
or you don't, you recognize the words
or they are just
                    a lot of letters on a page.
Maybe it's not too late
to reconstruct the burning.

POEM WITH HIDDEN MEANINGS THAT, AS A CHILD, YOU ALWAYS FEARED

The clouds conceal a beautiful story:
damselflies mating in a porcelain tub
filled with pearly bubbles. Copy
the pose of an observer:
                              the animal
sees you stuffing your kids' throats
with hot dogs; the animal takes
a finger from your child's hand.

I learn a lot from sitting
on this little stool—that it's complicated
to chronicle the ways rust becomes
distraction. It's complicated to explain
plaid. How do you convey *ruby*
or *puritan* or *lubricate?*
In the limited language of now
there's only one idea—
                              be happier
than you were the moment before.
Make peace with your own jugular.

Somewhere a pianist warms her hands
by a fire, holds the morning
in her palms, watches it stretch
then vanish into the ripening sun.
It's the visible plan of a garden
before it runs into itself
that signifies intention.
You can turn me into ash—
hold me until I become transparent.

WHEN BRAINS CONSIDER THE FUTURE

Nests of rubbish and grass, there
on the unfinished concrete supports

of the bomb-proof building,
provide protection from predators

though as often as these pigeons
reproduce, one could hardly kill them

off, since they're just crooing
into the window, watching

our work get done. There's no way
to rid ourselves of them,

and it's been tried—pesticides,
noise, fire—they resettle

themselves calmly back on the nest,
and I am counting their eggs,

thinking a pigeon-egg omelette
might be just the thing to exact

a little retribution for all
the thought I've spent on them

in these last years, over the moans
of my conscience, flicking cigarettes

into their nests, spraying air freshener
out at them, though they're just

out of reach and it can hardly be
more than a momentary disturbance.

They have settled here, as I have,
and do not mean to leave,

not even with the singeing
of feathers or the loss of a few eggs

to secure a concrete future here
on the building's ledge, and in a way,

I, too, refuse to leave, am walking
toward it in nothing but

my belted raincoat to meet my future
husband, though for now he's

just a hot date and I'm risking
what I think I must to please him—

what woman would think of making love
anywhere but in a soft bed,

her backside cushioned by Serta,
her hair kept from ruin

by pillows? It's men who want
to couple in doorways and cars,

their natures spelling the test
of romance. No, I was thinking

of the places I lay down,
then stood up from being spread

over an office chair, wanting
one session of crazy love

in the ruins of ceremony.
It is true that my back

has known the surfaces of desks,
that the toes of my shoes

hold that building's carpet fibers,
the same fibers, no doubt, that

grace the nests of the pigeons,
the same discomfort borne for stability

and the feel of something solid
beneath the feet, behind the back.

Blue Moon

February comes like ice, slips down
and covers everything. It is the minute
after midnight, the blue moon still
hanging in the sky and us down here

going haywire, the tides and beaches
and bars, little pockets of frenzy
with no tabs to pay, but a few dollars
still in our wallets and one matchstick

striking down a shoe, even if the wood
is damp and the blue sulfur cap
flies across the room into someone's beer,
and the night is cold, so it's not impossible

to imagine you, there in the mountains
with your view of the purer air and your skin
signaling to me all across the country
that in another week we'll be touching

and running our warm tongues across
each other. I haven't spent one night
without your shadow. I haven't awakened
one morning without your voice inside

my head. They say the moon pulls
our emotions over us like an heirloom quilt,
and I'm buying it, believe the orbits
of matter mark us invisibly so that

we cover ourselves over and over, safe
in the tug and grasp of love
until one day we peek out, find
the pattern faded but still distinct, even

in the dark grays of evening when
the moon's light shines through the glass,
tracing our faces and shoulders, casting
our one shadow on the floor's slim boards.

DEVOTIONS IN CONFIDENCE

There's a word for what we do
when a moment passes, when
the incidentals of traffic

and mayhem don't bother us at all.
Aren't you willing to be blown an inch
or two into what the winds inspire?

I believe everything you will never say.
I'm holding my ticket and the spectrum
is reversed: sweet green

a red glow, sirens of moss,
bruise-leaves and hematoma grass.
My ribcage flutters under its negligée

of skin, breath falling hard
and entering another mouth.
All it would take would be this

strange colloquy of fur
and carapace and wing. Try thinking
of sidewinders and a sloe gin fizz,

or the gentleness of persimmons:
there is always a secret
that won't bear telling.

Or Else

Or else there were words
I did not understand,
protocol and *certainty,*
because the light came
suddenly and I was alone
on a corner of the world.
It was a moment
but it was longer, as long
as embarrassment or fear, or
blue tunnels where birds roost.
Or else there were plans
that fell to nothing, a scold
in time. The wind was a zipper
closing the trees. There
were places I could not bear
to go—roads, restaurants,
gardens. Sparrows refused
to fly. A scuffle through bones
could remind me of pebbles,
of brown decomposing brown.
The shell of memory washes
only once onto the beach.
Or else what I love
vanishes into the deepening night,
heightened by trains, a quilt
of thorns. Nothing happens
in dreams' uncomplicated light
where everything matters
a little—highway, barrio, brothel.

ANTITHESIS: THE GARDEN OF HYSTERIA

I am nurturing a bonsai tree, cataloging
its senseless growth and lactations.

Something has caused me to desire
milk, to see whiteness as a pure tonic.
I believe I can make a single idea
into noise: there are ways I'll become

myself, my skin will correct me.
My spine will remember how to turn
into itself. I return to the house

that's a web. I try to recall.
Anything I wanted was stitched into me
with a thick rope, objects that owned color

and blood. A young girl selling marzipan
carries me to a distant port: this dry garden
turned to paradise though the air is parched
so everything dries in an instant.

Clothes stiffen on the lines, trees beg and bury
their roots deep. Here are anxious latitudes.

Here is brown dominion. Did I want baseball cards
and chewing gum, weeds to brush

the backs of my calves? Maybe it was silence
I wanted: in the early days they thought
that the womb wandered around the body.

What wandered was my attention,
my ability to focus on someone
as long as he desired me. Meaning

was the sound of bees that vibrated
through me, either nauseated violence
or intricate fabric. From the rim of a canyon

came a wind. From the crest of the wind
came prophecy. The wind ran through me.
Call me hysterical—

it's the snap that comes when I want
to creep back into myself, but someone
prevents me. If counting is required,

I have toes. If love is required, I have
my two hands, four yards of skin.

SKIN

The underside of the toad
makes me think of plastic,

of exotic purses gathering heat
at the weekly market. Across a white wall

the sun casts graffiti worthy of the best
tagging in L.A. or New York, conflicting claims

of light and shadow. To know an animal,
study what's closest to the ground:

pads of the feet, claws, sloping belly,
what came out last from the soup.

Better, look it in the eye, trace
the angle to the earth.

You'll have to spend some
time repairing stories

that have frayed, postures
you can no longer hold,

though any statue
can imitate a human pose.

What's more difficult than to be
a real live girl, to have

to wipe yourself and blow your nose?
There are roads to follow

that will go somewhere.
What's left to save here anyway?

A barnacle clinging to the shell's best side,
paramour and provider, ornament

altering the water's flow.
Still, the rest of us smile,

arms akimbo, and hover an inch above
the street. We'll wait until it rises,

until the air shimmers pine blue, particle
and wave, like the sky

in a photograph.
Freedom from the astrolabe,

liberty from dust
and panic, the due-North,

down-home astronomy of love—
just point me in a direction.

Where something needs to be said. Some passage
opens in the day's high heat, path

to a garden, tranquil
as a virus that's learned mutation.

Evil is always confident
small fugues

of good won't last.
It's time

to import something really new, a way
to distill thinking down

to pure thought that takes a shape
and defines what a word has become—

the ghostliness of the individual brain,
where you can find a silhouette

of complexity, but not ideas
in the round. Look again

at the toad's underbelly,
at the patterns of flame,

of mountains and highways embracing
a spot on a tree.

If not, the words *animal* and *niche*
are useless

relics, embers cooling
in the last days

of one particular summer
when we discovered the meanings

but didn't write them down, so
they've vanished like the skin

we used to have
when we were very young.

OBSESSIONAL

I have an obsession with the color red,
with the insides of my eyes, with the burning
streak of sky that signals
it is morning. Make a clean break

when you first see skin:
there is a bandage here, a fishhook,
a skein of violet yarn.

I am obsessed with corn, and the husks
of corn, with the yellow of bees

and pineapples and lemons.
At a cemetery, five hundred candles
burn under wood and glass and iron.
One color arrives everywhere: gray
mountain, gray sky, and all day

it tries to rain. The air prevents sound.
When I am on a train, I am obsessed
with the train, with strange murmurings

and steel that bends around sound.
Then I am obsessed with sound.

I am obsessed with obsession—I am—
it's my only vice, beyond smoking
and drinking and sex. I am forlorn
at not being obsessed, when archetype
replaces occurrence. Still, I am over

my obsession with love. I have become
obsessed with drama: I walk among
the dynamite and hydrangea, and live.

Manifesto

I know that dying is how we escape
the rest of our lives. I think that trees
send us a message: do not believe

you are lucky. The skins of apples
and the peeler will marry; it's simply
a question of when. Believe

in mourning and carrion birds.
Look how their fleshy treasures
dissolve in the sun before their very eyes.

To love something
you must have considered what it means
to do without. You must have thought

about it—the coefficient of the body
is another body—but do not forget
that there are people who are willing

to staple your palm to your chest.
Know there are places it isn't wise to go.
Begin again if you must: there are ways

to make up for what you have been before,
the dust in the corners that collects you.
Sympathy is overrated.

Rethink how lack
becomes everyone's master, drives us
into town and spends our money.

Quiet: the trees are napping.
Water meets itself again.
We reach for the days that precede us

and the world keeps us from knowing
too much. The body loves music,
the abandoned road of it;

each day a peel
lengthens in the shadow of blossoms,
fabric weaves itself into light.

Pay attention to the patterns. They repeat—
terraces erode, groves lie fallow—
order is cognate of joy.

In Memory of Freud

The motion of water is a lie, *we* are what moves
over *it,* to Brindisi or Lisbon,
faces on a ferry looking

at the silver bangles
the water wears.
You missed the beginning when

we were water
and light. What you always believed
you knew is a mistranslation.

No one wants to say
what has really been said. Stand
at the edge of the cliff

to remember whales and water buffalo,
signet rings and stone. Walk out to the pier.
Take in the length

of our yearnings. We were never meant
to walk over water. We were
meant to immerse ourselves

and recall how to move. Go back
in time to beyond time: what were you
doing when minerals formed?

Go back some more and tell me this fossil
is a bone that was your hand.
Maybe you are missing the chapter on Plague

or the chapter that tells you not to
practice in public what you secretly anoint.
These are episodes in the story, not the whole

story, so think of love
and loss as twins that argue then make up
when the air parts

and produces a grammar
of solitude. If the symbol
of longing

is a wire that winds
the circumference of the earth,
you must get on your knees.

*Thus in the beginning the world was so made
that certain signs come before certain events.*

—CICERO, *De Divinatione.* i. 118

ONE SUNDAY EACH SPRING

So quickly we're transported, the field a yellow cathedral:
    the strict rows of daffodils riffle up a pollen breeze,
        the barn yawns another annotation,

and the farmhouse, distant, tiny, props itself
    against the sky. Never mind that now the gentle mounds
        are left untilled, or that the farm, idle

for years, produces nothing but the remembrance
    of itself. Each April those old bulbs fracture
        again, all the pedicels again support glorious blooms,

and I am dressed up: pink gingham, patent leather,
    an empty Easter basket slung over my six-year-old arm.
        All the trees pass in furious motion—green touches glass,

the road narrows to dirt, then dead-end, and our family
    erupts from the car—we spend an hour
        working up the rows. See my nose, dusted yellow,

disappointed again each year when there's no aromatic reward
    from these flowers cultivated for size and number.
        Hear my hands slide down the hollow stalks,

my squeal at the eerie squeak of the stems as I pull.
    Feel the crust of mud caking my Mary Janes, the soles now
        moon-boot sized and heavy-stepping. Rains

must have moved across the state's southern tip
    last night, left the land too wet; we struggle
        to stitch ourselves into the rows, our arms still

flexing mechanically, a rhythmic clutch and transfer.
    And we find it is enough. The car fills with a brown
        odor of earth top-noted by green and yellow,

with wet newspaper, with the stems' weepy milk, and all
    of what rises again from the farm, the disappearing
        road, the last uneasy visit to the empty tomb of that field.

A Nap Sounded Good

this afternoon, so I lay on the sofa and dreamed
of generations of peoples, all working hard,
some harder than others, but everyone
harder than I. Take the Temple
of the Magician, which must have been hell
to construct there on that hot hill

at Uxmal, which means "three
times built," so three times the work.
I'd have made a bad Mayan. A bad
Egyptian, too, too lazy to measure each flood
with a nilometer, and the more land
that flooded, the more land was taxed.

And in Lepcis, I would have become dehydrated,
too lethargic to collect my salt cakes.
I'm bad at drawing, so making portolan charts
to find harbors would have been out,
as would illustrating manuscripts
or tinting temple columns or painting frescoes.

Even the cave paintings at Santimamine, just
outlines, really, would have stretched
my limited skill. I wouldn't have done well
carving mammoth bone into a fertility figure,
or chert into a knife, and certainly that
massive Giza project would have worn me down.

And, being a girl, I couldn't have worked there.
I'd have, no doubt, been collecting winkles
on the coast of Japan, filling a skin bag
with hot clay chunks to cook raw food,
or roasting Bogong moths, all to feed
myself and the family I'd have had.

But I don't see myself doing any of that.
It's more my vision that I helped invent
something: Linear B, a method
for weaving palm frond mats,
impressed brick, Greek coins, delicate ink,
a way to harness fire, the wheel.

THERA

I stand in the sun, my body red and slow
from moving all day from one dig to another.
I've come to the city of Akrotiri, where the flow

of lava through this Bronze Age town covered
everything: clay pots, the still-bright frescoes of swallows
and lilies, the rhytons used in worship. It was rediscovered

less than thirty years ago when the cliffside hollows
began to sink, a little at first, then more, until the slope
was pitted with holes. The road to the excavation follows

the lip of a cliff, where the sea glows blue against the taupe
of the landscape, and the bus is more stifling on this ride
than the inland journeys of the days before, when no hope

of sea air, or a quick swim, or ripe cherries at the roadside
distracted me. Here, their rituals seem as clear
as ours. The stone streets angle past gray ash, stratified

by three thousand years and chemistry. Where timbers were,
only impressions of the wood remain, and we know
what rooms they used for cooking and for bathing, and where

they slaughtered goats, for an offering table stands alone
in a corner, a hole at one end for the blood to leak.
By day's end all the fractured pottery thrown

to the edges of the rooms, the ash, and the frescoes work
into knots that we can scarcely untangle, though
the sun begins its usual descent, its slow, red arc.

To a Friend Who Moved Away

Summer, falling into the day's heat,
a pack of Marlboro's in my coat.
It's the beginning
of a fine story. I could tell you

how I once imagined all the surfaces
of payphones had been treated
with a special dust that would glow
under black light. Everyone would know

exactly where I had been: I was learning
the upholstery of a '72 Thunderbird.
I memorized the tufts and stitching
that imprison the back seat.

I was learning how to lie,
or how to lie back, and take in
the details. You were drawing in
those details and exhaling them

as the ashes of graphite.
Pencil drawings of everyday objects,
the walls' walls, a cell inside a cell
depicting another world where you weren't

as lonely and I wasn't so much
far away as I was just outside
the perimeters, and likely to come in
at any time. Any time. Now. And then,

of course, there would be
more to the story, if you were here
for me to tell it to. You would know
who moved into your old colonial

and what color the trees still turn
each fall, and when to drive
the back roads in southern Illinois
looking for the farm where peacocks balance

on the ramshackle roof and call out
noisily to the cars to move on,
to leave them alone and without
the engine's rumbling to put them off

their feed. You would know
that when I got out of high school
I moved to Baltimore, then California.
You would know about the dream

I used to keep having about our street
and the streetlight that isn't there
in waking, and the figure who stands
just beyond the light's yellow halo,

and that your old neighbors' daughter
died in May, that the son
of the old couple way down the hill
moved them to a nursing home last year.

Most of the people you knew have died
or moved and been lost
to distance or lethargy.
That vanishing is something like a fever,

no clear beginning or end, just some point
at which one is undeniably sure
of nothing. Of the two of us, you
were the luckier. But I am still here,

and today I was thinking I wish
I knew where you were.
If I did, I'd tell you how I swore
I'd never lose touch, though your name

disappeared years ago from my address books,
the space under "L" inkless, untouched
by all these things, and two more:
we forgive the dead everything,
and whatever we neglect is free to disappear.

THE BREAKERS

Eight years of a half-hour a day
    yet all I can play now is one
        tune, "The Breakers," a scale

exercise that's beautiful, though
    far less complex
        than what I could play well

when I quit lessons at fourteen,
    when I found a horse
        more interesting than ivory

and pedals, the mucking out
    of stalls to keep me busy
        and strong, and grooming,

cleaning tack, riding the ring,
    on the trails, across the stream,
        down by the pig farm that

in summer smelled almost
    evil, though the pigs seemed
        to smile, waving curly tails,

stomping around, sending more
    scent into the air, waiting
        to be bacon or a holiday ham,

and we'd ride past, on the way
    to going back, after the sunset
        dictated we turn around and

return just as the chords in
    "The Breakers" repeated after
        a long run of new, just as

almost anything turns
    into a pattern once it's run
        out of starting, and begun

to seem similar to itself,
    again, even in the last light
        of a summer afternoon, when

sticky corn waits in a drum,
    the curry comb cramps
        the hand, and the saddle blanket

needs to air on the fence
    before it can be put away
        by these hands that knew

a lot of songs, as well as
    the mistakes you had to make
        to learn them, but chose

the living thing over
    the beautiful keys faced
        in the carved tusks

of elephants, whom I'd
    also probably rather have ridden,
        given the choice.

In Which I Time-Travel at the End of the Twentieth Century

Back, brain: to the caul of adolescence,
to the wanderings of hormones
and to hemispheres shifting.

The sun loiters behind the clouds—
when I turn on the radio,
I'm tracked by bad songs

from years ago. Waitresses scowl
at weary customers.
I couldn't put myself in your way

to save you, couldn't catch the bullet
that passed. The only way
of looking at the lung is after

it's no longer needed,
its clean, pink music, enchanting
if you're seventeen, your senses

skewed from the brevity
of experience. And wasn't beauty
what this was about all along?

Strange that this late crows
can still catch my eye,
so even when

the briefcase and the steering wheel
point me toward the office,
even when my vows have been made,

even when an aerial view of the plats
and valleys of this life would show
a clear path, obvious and easy,

I still meander near the unsure courses
that present themselves off to one side—
seductive—perhaps even possible.

Take my case as every woman's
who ever listened to promises.
Believed them. Thought them true.

The prediction is always
for the sun to set and rise,
for the seasons to change,

for meaning to sneak up, rather
than present itself in front.
I believe this with every cell.

Project Cover-Up

In that late 60's craze, almost none of our furniture was spared,
  not my already vintage burled walnut dresser, not the metal
    steamer trunk where my brother stashed his cigarettes,

not even our Kimball upright, which forever after beckoned us
  to practice by extending a folksy avocado hand.
    It was the time of antiquing—each faux-finish the result

of kits from Lloyd's Hardware and my mother's labor
  while atypically clad in denim, marked with the stigmata
    of crafts, her skin, her clothes dappled with stain.

It was the time of papers routinely spread out to protect
  cement from what was drying and catch what dripped, the ivory
    bullets that splattered down headlines on patios and driveways

across America and blanched the troop movements
  and protests and body counts and lies, and while our house filled
    with lightened versions of recognizable things, a day later

the paper was balled up and stuffed in the trash, having served
  its purpose. We wasted lots of things then—the masking tape
    that protected the hardware, the square of fake cheesecloth

the kit provided to swipe the stain across the paint's surface,
  rectangles of sandpaper. Even the box the kit came in, more
    package than product, suggested how posh the results could be.

Think of every surface newly old and the heady scent of varnish,
  an atmosphere steeped in wealth, the piano glistening and amber
    light gracing the dresser's finish, imagine how fresh

each project looked. Oh, there were cautions: the temperature
  had to be just right. Wiping some in an eye could blind you.
    Whatever else the stuff came into contact with was ruined.

The effect was worth all the risk. A couple of years later
   the novelty had worn off. Stores pushed what could remove
      the layers, solvents that softened paint into a crackled mush

that could be putty-knifed away and would restore the raw surface.
   Cash registers rang and soft cloths were lifted, apace with
      all the vapors of suburbia rising again, holy and toxic.

HEARSAY

My brother always tells
the story of derailing the train:
we had only meant to flatten
the pennies we had piled twenty high
on the tracks, yet that day there came
screeching. Then, steam hissed
from the crippled train.

And, from the damaged hull came
seven monkeys, copper in the slices
of sun piercing the trees.
They'd been, he says, bound
for a zoo, and our pile of pennies
had bought them one taste
of Evanston, Illinois,
where our thrilled shrieks mingled
in the canopy with theirs.

That night, he says, even sleep
came wrapped in the howl
and flux of the rails—
as though the trains passing
could make us forget the nights
without them, or the repetition
of a story could make it nearly true.

CURE PORCHES

Long before I was born, my aunt Johanna caught
        galloping consumption. Her parents converted
        their verandah into a closed porch
where she could sleep in winter, breathe

Black Forest air. Rx : *Rest. Fresh air.*
        Nights, she and my father cuddled for warmth.
        At White Haven Sanatorium, the poor and very sick,
those almost dead, were moved to Shack I,

Department No. 3, but not before paying
        the state with work for their care
        while coughing up the blood and foul nodules
of the disease. *Graded exercise. Strychnia.*

At Saranac Lake the structures announce illness
        from the past. These homes were adapted
        so wealthy patients could take cure
in the Adirondacks' air, outside but sheltered.

Germicides by inhalation. Hydrotherapy.
        Innocuous planks and boards concealed all
        the accoutrements—disposable sputum cups
where tubercle bacilli collected, cure chairs

that placed one in the Fowler position, best
        in which to breathe, stone pigs filled
        with hot water to warm patients' feet.
Dr. Angney's gaseous enemas at the House of Mercy.

Sliding windows facing South were added to porches
        where owners rented space. But, Johanna. Not rich,
        she had lain for weeks in bed, wasting.
Liniments. Iron. The last morning

my father awakened to her body beside him.
      She endured experiments with serums and milk.
      She slept nearly outside, enveloped by dampness.
She defeated all the architecture.

NON SEQUITUR

These days, what comes from your mouth
often surprises. This afternoon I am
reading to you the biography
of Teddy Roosevelt, condensed
by *Reader's Digest,* yet expanded,
too, the light banking off the large print,

the pages glaring. My voice
keeps coming out hard, loud,
almost falling against itself.
I continue. I explain.
As though your childhood had come after
mine, as though the light
in this room had always bounced

off plastic liners and catheters.
I am angry how age is romanticized.
Angry that people don't talk
about incontinence or skin
that erases itself from
the constant weight of the body.

You are in bed, but I ask,
this third time, if you want to get up.
You're satisfied to know
you're already there, again.
It's some time later when you crook a finger.
You ask me to come closer. You whisper,
You could kill me in my sleep.

THE FISH CHANNEL

As you were dying, sometimes I went back
to the room to catch a nap or a shower.
I'd click on the television for an hour,
flip around the channels for lack

of anything to do but sit by your bed
and watch you breathe and breathe, that motion
your only language. Some kinds of devotion
may take more imagination than mine, bred

of simply wanting you to stay. Sitting
in front of the screen, watching the chain
of bubbles rise, tracking the plain
paths, became a kind of sedative, an unremitting

way to ease the coming loss. I knew nearly
nothing of death, of the way it rings in the numb
mind, chiming without end, or how some
of the brain's cells will seize on it, sincerely

and with the strength of the tides.
Channel 7 was its own ocean, a narcotic blue
square of water, the fish almost washed from view
by the lights behind them, and, near the sides,

the plants pulled and swayed against the water.
Often I imagined the whole hotel, all those sad,
grieving people, sitting at the edges of their beds,
staring at the Fish Channel at once. The water.

The bubbles. Fish pulsing across the screen.

Stepping into the River

I know what you'll do when I tell you
of grief, because you are a river,
able to hold the banks at bay, water
passing through on its way to the seas.

You are no stream, but the Colorado,
the Mississippi, a great force flowing.
Water is best left alone to speak
in unintelligible murmurs, to clean

the landscape and the soul, but the soul
is a small tin cup in a street vendor's
hand, filling with valuable things,
emptied when it's turned over,

and souls are the color red, silk-screened
and vigorous, the blood streaming down
a wounded soldier's leg.
Or they are feathers. It is insubstantial

to name the soul, to want
to possess your own or another's.
Let the Devil make his bargains.
Let grapefruit and cherries grow

by the sides of the roads so that when
you pass them they speak to you:
I am hungry to be color and light.
I have traveled from Boston,

from Miami, from San Francisco:
what herds us into the paddock
is not grief, but joy. You must open
your eyes. They are the color

of India ink, the color of snow,
industrial smoke prowling the dusk sky,
steam rising. There are possibilities
you've never considered: winter

is a heat so cold it warms you.
Love is a method to learn pain.
I am holding the crust of a warm piece
of bread, and tossing it into the river.

Take a hand into yourself, as if skin
were water, as if the fingers of a lake
gripped the land. You are outside
yourself in the moonlight.

Lexicographers know the way
to harness a river is to trace it to its source,
the sequential moments of arrival,
and then to enter the landscape.

You are wandering over the engraved stones,
the furrows and pits worn through
the years, the distinct marks that define
it as the seat of something, source
of all our troubles and our gifts.

For the Old Ones

Be glad you'll not have to spend eternity
sipping the blood of your enemies

from their skulls, since you've passed
the age of heroes and did not fall

in battle, though some would say
it's no disgrace to have escaped alive

by simple timing, and since one can't
control beginnings, one remains

blameless. You wove
the strands of your days into a strong

braid, into a river, into a story unlike
the garbled music blaring from nearby

radios; and if once the plan
or pattern shimmered indistinct before

you, now, in the later air, the dark
side of red becomes you.

Seems there is rapture in the pages
of the trees. Seems there is audience

and an orchestra of crows. Seems
the unmediated strain of summer passes

into crickets and mice. Listen to the bold
complaint of darkness so soon after

it agreed to the conditions: beauty resides
in clavicle and cartilage. Every

little alchemy is still a riddle never solved.
Your hands clasp each other, imitation

of prayer. Seems in the opinion of clouds
that the rain is running away from home.

❖

But it still moves.

—GALILEO

TRIAGE

It is a kind of triage, a setting
of priorities, this loving the bud
and hating the wilted flower: the red
of geraniums, another siren, another
little death resting in a bush, where
the air is different, the light
is different, the very molecules

we are, are different. All the stars
are out tonight, and I am spilling
salt, watching its crystals fall
into the patterns of stars, into
beautiful sadnesses. Vega, Sirius,
Alpha Centauri: I am wishing
on them until I run out of names.

It is the month of buds
and the vines begin their strangulations.
This life is a falling-away,
a discarding, though we collect
many things—our supplies of helium
and laughter are not in danger.
Still the end of winter turns

into itself: we must stay
in our own bodies, and though
we may leave cells on the pages
or on doorknobs we turn,
the stars keep turning out to be
only the idea of stars
before their light can reach us.

A Very Short History of Everything

Setting out on an adventure
the protagonist takes heart:

jimsonweed, boa constrictor,
the whine of small machinery.

A curtain draws across,
a healing wound.

Everyone is making up
premises. It is necessary.

A shaker of salt, an empty
cage, a mourning dove: make

of these what is missing.
If making promises delays you,

cross over and tell me
a story of heat, the ways

to provide it. Cross back.
You'll know the way.

An evening out, a dislocation.
Someone has marked the exits.

Someone has numbered the seats.
There is little in this world

that won't capture
someone's attention—acanthus,

red brick, bulldozers mixing
the earth. One trouble

with always is now, how
a body turns from itself.

There are laws: a body at rest
remains at rest and so on—

energy can be transformed
but not created or destroyed—

first law of thermodynamics
and also of love. Metaphor

will only carry you
so far, and the sky always

the same, same blue.
Startled birds rising,

any kind of harness,
a cage of water. Go back

to what came before, the corset,
the arrow, rancid meat hanging

in a square. Is this
where you want to live and die?

On the Natures of Matter and Time

It's no use pining over how advanced the world
has become—take the remote control out
of your children's hands. They love
technology more than they love
imagination, that old companion turned dim

and sad. It's no use wondering where time
has gone, why the seasons shorten
and the muscles grow slack, why tire pressure
and blood pressure must be measured
and recorded and known. It's no use

organizing the half-hour slots we live in,
no use erasing the appointments
from the book, and even if we could
turn the Etch-a-Sketch
screen over, gray out the space, we'd know

there's little time. No use crawling the walls,
paying bills on time, or lowering your
mortgage rate. You mustn't think love.
It's no use holding a syllable on your tongue
or believing in altruism.

Outside the lamplight, under
a skin of dust, it's no use wondering
what kind of brain crackles beneath
your skull, just as it's no use monitoring
the banana's peel for signs of decay.

No use trying on clothes that cover
your body and protect you from
the blatant stares of gentlemen, and
no use laughing when the future becomes
caught up in what's called the now.

You've made choices and signed things.
You've driven to a lonely spot
on a dark road. You've lit a fire
with kindling and log. It's no use clapping
the bellows and sending up prayers.

Your past will keep you warm.
No use creaming corn
or forging iron. Things are already
the shapes they want to be. No use
pinching the candystriper or bending

a child across your knee. All we need
to know is enacted by mercury,
Humpty-Dumpty, by broken glass
glinting in the dark: once something
breaks apart, it's a new thing, forever

and ever, until it breaks apart again
into something else. It's no use dividing
the world into broken and unbroken, whole
and part, healthy and sick. It's no use
crying: your tears become drops. Just water.

On the Nature of Interrogatives

I'm on my fourth gin and tonic
when I realize the answer
to most questions I've ever
asked or answered is pretty
close to the same: *Of course/*

of course not. Each serves
equally well if you're asked
if you've already eaten lunch,
or whether that clock is correct,
or if the burning smell coming

from the kitchen is something
we all need to be alarmed about.
You know the answers
to the other questions—square
root of 64, the number of

angels unfortunate enough
to spend all their time proving
that ridiculous head-of-a-pin
question—even if they come
to you in vague flashes and

squeeze out from your brain
the recipe for your grandmother's
lasagna, or all those admonitions
not to ride motorcycles without
a helmet, even if the struggle

to recite them causes the seventh
dwarf's name to slide into
the abyss of nonremembrance
forever. It's only our bad luck
that the questions are changing,

that you're just as likely
to be asked about communicable
diseases as what type of dog
you had when you were ten, as
that one query almost everyone

gets around to—just how fast
you can finish something—even
if the right question would be
to ask if you could manage it
at all, if you could perform

the miracle of completion well,
rather than quickly, well enough
to want to sign your name
where no one will have to ask
Who did that? Where can I
find another one just like it?

On the Nature of Incredulity

It was a morning that sang like any morning
when there's bright sun
and little chance that the ripening peaches will not

arrive at the market,
or that the gold spray paint isn't in stock, because
later, you plan to wander

indiscriminately down each and every alley
in this town, gilding
garages and fences, tagging garbage cans and cars,

because they called
last night to inform you, to let you know that
Columbus sighted land,

that the printing press is now in use,
that electricity has been
invented. Over the roar of an anachronism, they want

you to know that
plumbing is now a possibility. Maybe there's no need
anymore of a saddle

for the brontosaurus, since we've reached a crisis point
in the retelling
of our stories—you won't get far if you concentrate

on the U.S. Open
or an alternative cure for syphilis. It pays to remember
our time is limited,

and benefactors, few. Where's the last place
you prayed?
The last time I prayed was years ago,

and only when
I thought I might lose one of my eyes. Nothing
less than the loss

of sight could make me approach thinking
that prayer
might help. Such an elegant solution requires

a less figurative
problem: the dying of frogs, the dirtying of oceans.
If it only took

a gesture to reverse the solid actions of centuries,
we'd all be doing it.
We'd be doing it by committee. We'd be pledging

support, mailing
back our little pre-paid envelopes with our hefty
checks inside.

Intuitive Motions

Then I had an affection for the unfamiliar, for what burned
and what was submerged in shallow waters.
        Everything unknown carried the same fascination:

a marble bench still as a lone tooth in the mouth of a dim park,
the brush of calligraphy, the small secret wish.
        But some modesty held it all back. A curtain

blew around me. So I understood their culture before I collided
with it. I had learned the traditions of drifters.
        Had I been uncertain, or left behind among them,

everything I needed could be found in their names
which wrapped themselves around the jugular,
        or in the certainty of their gestures. There

the dark spots of my nature descended into view, and the ways
in which the year parsed itself—season, month,
        day, minute—were my anachronisms. Take history.

You can't plan how wars resolve or the outcome of famine.
        But you can create a tableau that conforms to the facts,
            then indulge in conjecture. Moreover, I began to think

of people in terms of inventions. This woman would know
the divinity of trains. That man would calculate
        how to cross the impassable river. This young girl

would administer the one vaccine. These are merely everyday
objects from my time—habits, mechanical weather
        to pass us from one generation into the next.

There are infrequent surfacings and vanishings.
        Intermittent chronicles and gossip. Fragments of a story,
            lingering. There must be such legends.

Songs begin with the composer's commitment to order.
   Find any ancient author: the tempo of history
            has narrowed to a slow and circuitous creek.

Along its banks, among the notes that remain, are others,
   cast aside, their cadences disappearing. People stand
            on those banks as if they too were notes slipping

into that vortex. There will be no vaccine. The trains
   have stopped making their runs. There is no bridge
            over that river to join these lockets of land.

OBJECTS AND WEATHERS

Until the beginning of summer
it's cool here, cooler than where I'm from,
and over-landscaped, sprinklers clicking
on each morning to coax plants

imported from elsewhere into blooming,
covering the dirt with green throws,
fringed at the edges,
an occasional tulip

or daffodil. Under the threat of drought
water tastes better, even somehow wetter,
a silk cord dangling in the throat.
Somewhere it may be practical to count

on thunder, but here storms whisper
right by; they drop dry rains and move on.
I'm keeping the time I've saved
in an amber box. I can see it

inside, trapped, an ancient insect
caught doing what it did: ticking
by and disappearing
into the hourglass neck.

If I were braver, I'd open the box,
take back an hour and live it
again, repetitive motion
and an aftershock,

like an echo of a deed
I'm hearing again.
History allows for no such thing:
Once and only

once, then the door closes, tight.
No novelty in doing things again,
anyway, so maybe it is best after all
to keep the lid down, to watch time cuddle

with itself. But what if you
rediscovered relativity or the catapult?
You could amaze yourself
with the fundamentals of geometry, forecast

the returns of comets. I am deaf
to other dimensions, know how
truly stuck I am
in this here and this now.

I know I can't relive the hours
I've spent daydreaming out the window,
just as I know I can't know more
than the sum of all discovery,

figured on its best day. But almost
every object is the product
of one single mind—someone dreamed up
the disposable diaper,

the traffic light, the little doggy coat.
Someone decided. Made. Their time
lost or spent in perfect clarity: I want
the world to have this.

It's a gift, an irrevocable promise
that we won't have to do without
TV dinners or Q-tips or in-ground sprinklers,
without the vacuum cozy,

not ever, until the skies darken and pull
the last bit of heat
from our planet,
and there is nothing left to have.

A FEW COWS IN A LANDSCAPE

The movies depict them flying upside down,
or swatting their tails while grazing
and gazing languorously, but I know
they'd rather be dancing with each other

on that far sloping hill, hoof
to flank to shoulder, lashes dipping
into flirt, so I want them to walk
into view in tuxes and gowns, upright,

twirling together, moving into waltz,
because I like it when the wind's jazz
plays over the fields, when the fence
bows in courtly gesture. I know the wind

blows pieces of other heres
into this one, that there shouldn't be
too much to finding a mote of Ohio dust
in our Kentucky coffee, but there is,

and we spend all our lives trying
to send it back: a grain
of sand from Nantucket, a speck
of dirt from Albany. We know the world

is remaking itself as we know the way
our face should look on any morning
in any mirror. Copperheads
and rattlesnakes carry some of that

dirt on their bellies, spread it
across town, across the country.
A bit of mud from a Georgian's shoe
flakes off when a plane touches down

in Seattle, or when the wind rides itself from
the North, and what good are the words *cow*
or *home* or *wind* unless there's this evidence
that it can spread everywhere, blow into us?

A Few Words to the Carnivores

Suppose a thumbtack of wax. Suppose
an empty grave and a cormorant's nest.

Dormant creeds, I wish you the heavy litmus
of faith. To the left, a sprig. To the right,

a rotting apple. Like the woodpecker's tongue,
these gossipy nights start and start again.

Then I was watching the birds: tern,
jackdaw, sparrow, crow, a posse

lifting itself toward migrations. Still the light
passes through us on its way to the earth.

Someone once told me empathy is a simple dressing
for a complex wound. You must take

someone's heart and caress it.
Suppose electricity. Suppose the texture

of an eel, the texture of the aorta.
Suppose we are something more than meat.

Vanishing Point

The way an island holds back
water, faith lets us forget
for awhile that everything

we are and have is brief
and less than an isthmus
connecting us to the next

plane. It is a winter afternoon,
and the trees' branches reach
down to touch the snow, to

sample the ground. One
of these syncopations
of weather will startle

the seasons into change, so
don't try to tell time by
scale or fin, the iridescent

motion of the tides.
Everything is heavier than
it appears to be on earth,

and the swans would be
lifted by the slightest wind
into white kites that flare

in the sky against the trees'
branches, were it not
for the miracle of gravity,

which is really sorrow,
keeping us grounded.

POEM FROM ACROSS THE COUNTRY

The flowers have checked their suitcases.
In the old mythology, flowers could speak:
Day moves across the meadow;

autumn shadows break our necks.
In the waiting room of the heart
we all sit against the walls and read

outdated magazines. Something looks
over the shoulders of the crowd
and beckons: maps end

the curiosity we must have had
about time; crossings plotted
are no adventure.

It is always like this. Suits and skirts
walking themselves to their stations,
another penny spent and rolling

under the wheels' economy.
One by one we are called
and we go, but I can see,

even with the image of hypnotic light
that paralyzes me when my eyes close:
another day is gone.

Is is; Is isn't.
One of these is true.
I thirst; there is no water.

Mind the oases of desire that fling
themselves at your throat, butterflies
committing suicide against your throat.

You won't have come
upon it yet, but it is there.
There must be a way to lose yourself

now, to resist cartography
and physics. How much
can it hurt to swallow

loss? I looked and was burned,
a heliotrope turning to track
the sun across my mind,

wanting it
to heat me so that I didn't
burn from the inside out.

PERMANENT RECORD

They sit in the dark recesses of drawers all over
 the world, a card, a half sheet of paper, recording
  the facts of the day the train jumped the rails

or when she stayed in bed too long or forgot to water
 the fern and a pair of drunken friends in rare form
  slipped on the drying leaves scattered on the floor.

Unsatisfactory. The varied, curling scripts go on:
 she passed out pills in class . . . more than once she threw
  down objects . . . she was once arrested in a small town

in a large state . . . she drove away from a car she had hit
 without telling anyone or leaving even a note. *Criminal.*
  She stole recipes and garments and men, promised to bring

pennies back to trusting clerks who never saw her
 again. *Past Due.* She looked out windows at just
  the wrong times, saw injustices and what else the world

offers. She helped her husband choose his tie each morning,
 taught the neighbor's child how not to bite. *Very Good.*
  Under the pots she liked to light a fire, watch it

change into goblins. She talked on the phone too much,
 of things she must have known would hurt—history or love,
  and death, big things reduced to words that scarcely

said anything. *Guilty.* Her vision cleared. She slept more
 than a third of it all away, pined over losses that weren't,
  really. She inverted the seasons and betrayed the tribe.

Condemned. She noticed signs she couldn't read,
and went the way the arrows pointed. Her choices were eloquent
and strange. She didn't when she could have. *Balance Due.*

She was happy sometimes. She looked up and down, found
what was there, then moved it to where it is now. She wanted it
to last. They balance out, perhaps, the *Goods*

and *Needs Improvements* that now fill nearly half the space.
But she made some things that sang. And she didn't want
to say too much. What blanks are left remain.

Under the Scorpion's Heart

What I was reaching for
was a handle, a brick,

or a gun, so I didn't notice
the sky darken to black canvas.

I didn't notice the rain.
I sat on the steps

and let the light obscure me.
There are places

I'll remember as kindling,
where centrifugal force

drives everything from the center,
and nothing I've ever heard

is true. What if the mud dries
to mirage, and there is no door

by which to leave?
The surf entangles

the logic of the sun,
but sadness is no answer.

Take into my mouth
the constellations of lemons,

and—as feathers presume water
and wind—make up my mind to rise.

ANOTHER OSMOSIS

The moon in its coma of sky rests
        there until the light's no longer right,
until the sun's forceps tear it from view.
                It's simple, really: the eyepiece of the microscope
allows one small sphere of vision: the circle
        you can see, the circle you extrapolate
into the rest of the world. Take from this: night.
        Take from this: champagne.
Take camel and corpus callosum.
        Feel a vow of scent surrounding.
Take from what you can't see: what you can.
        What you can.
What you can feel and touch and taste, what you can hear and
        also what you can smell, what lodges
in the limbic brain, honey
        and cactus—sweet prickly afterworlds
erasing themselves into surroundings.
        I'm sitting on nothing, on a pillow of nothing,
far up in the willow of memory: take from.
        Take from that: this.
Take from this: that voice.
        That voice that calls
that voice that calls from inside: come.
        Inside the envelope, inside the womb,
inside the arches of memory, you can hold on.
        You can take from the specimens of decay
the living circle, the voice,
        the sea rising on a tide of discretion.
The house disappears in a parody of mist.
        The seahorse rocks on its currents.
A mouth opens to enshroud sound,
        to evoke the sea, to evoke arches rising
and falling into the last of the miles of the journey,
        the spoken word, at last, rising
up and risen, alone on the tongue,
        and lifted, and then: song.

My thanks to everyone who's read one or more versions
of this book, especially Jack Vespa. Thanks, also, to
The MacDowell Colony, the Virginia Center for the Creative
Arts, and the Fundacíon Valparaíso in Spain, as well as the
Utah Arts Council, for encouragement while I was working
on these poems. Finally, I owe a special debt to my brother,
Erich Schilpp, who sometimes becomes my memory.